Big and Small

Julie Murray

Abdo Kids Junior
is an Imprint of Abdo Kids
abdobooks.com

Abdo
OPPOSITES
Kids

abdobooks.com

Published by Abdo Kids, a division of ABDO, P.O. Box 398166, Minneapolis, Minnesota 55439.
Copyright © 2019 by Abdo Consulting Group, Inc. International copyrights reserved in all countries.
No part of this book may be reproduced in any form without written permission from the publisher.
Abdo Kids Junior™ is a trademark and logo of Abdo Kids.

Printed in the United States of America, North Mankato, Minnesota.

102018

012019

Photo Credits: iStock, Minden Pictures, Shutterstock

Production Contributors: Teddy Borth, Jennie Forsberg, Grace Hansen

Design Contributors: Christina Doffing, Candice Keimig, Dorothy Toth

Library of Congress Control Number: 2018945730

Publisher's Cataloging-in-Publication Data

Names: Murray, Julie, author.

Title: Big and small / by Julie Murray.

Description: Minneapolis, Minnesota : Abdo Kids, 2019 | Series: Opposites |
    Includes glossary, index and online resources (page 24).

Identifiers: ISBN 9781532181771 (lib. bdg.) | ISBN 9781532182754 (ebook) |
    ISBN 9781532183249 (Read-to-me ebook)

Subjects: LCSH: Synonyms and antonyms--Juvenile literature. | Polarity--Juvenile
    literature. | Size perception--Juvenile literature. | Size and shape--Juvenile literature.

Classification: DDC 428.1--dc23

Table of Contents

Big and Small

A blue whale is big. It is the biggest animal in the world.

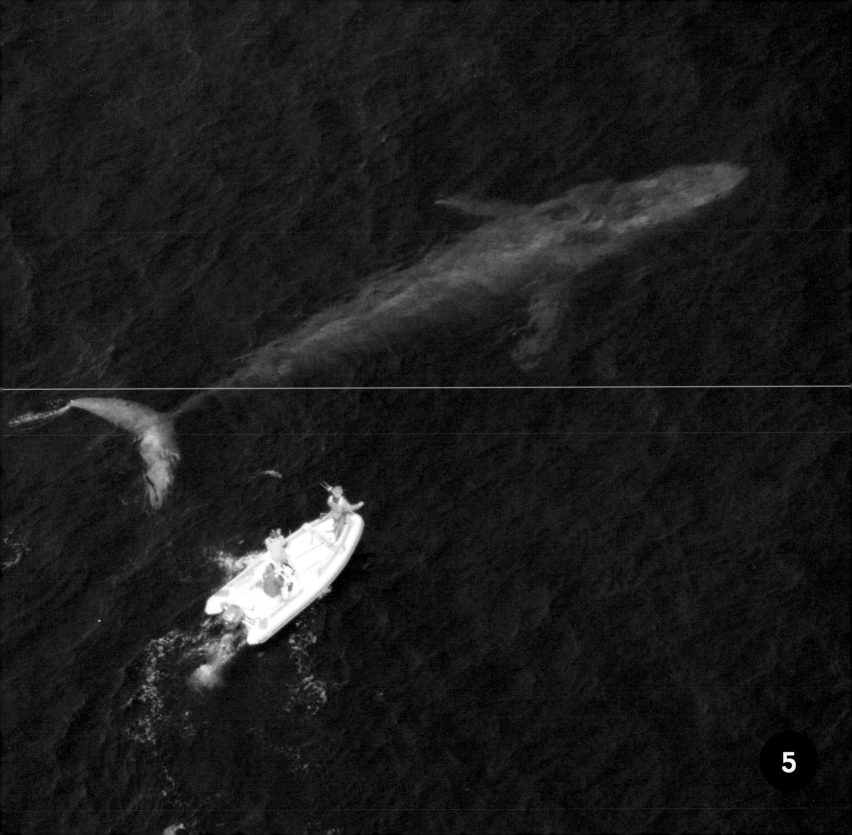

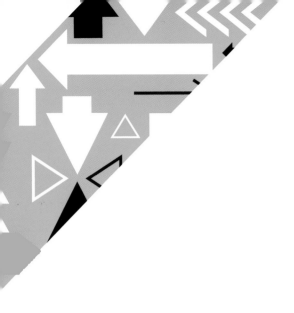

An ant is small. One is on
Sam's hand.

Some dogs are big. A Great
Dane is a very big dog!

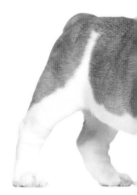

9

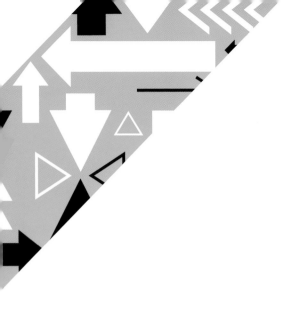

Some dogs are small. Anna's Yorkie sits on her lap.

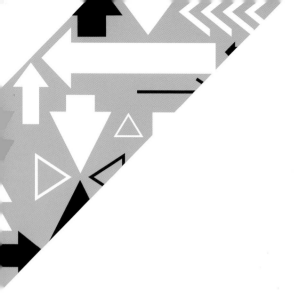

A bald eagle is big. Its **wingspan** is 7 feet (2.1 m)!

13

A hummingbird is small.
It is only 2 to 4 inches
(5-10 cm) long.

Some trees are big. The coast **redwoods** are the biggest.

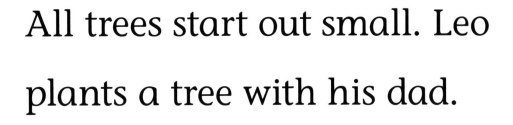

All trees start out small. Leo plants a tree with his dad.

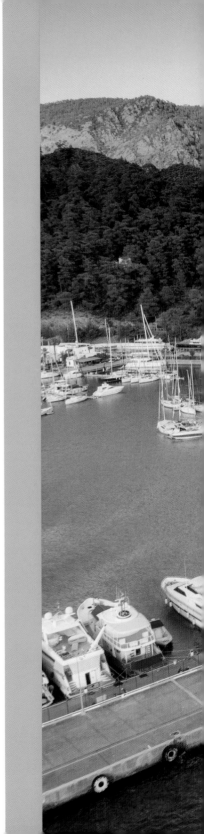

Look around you. What do you see that is big? What do you see that is small?

More Things Big and Small

big ball

big cat

big lollipop

small ball

small cat

small lollipop

Glossary

redwood
a very tall evergreen tree found in
northwestern North America.

wingspan
the distance from the tip of one
wing of a bird to the tip of the other.

Index

Abdo Kids
ONLINE
FREE! ONLINE MULTIMEDIA RESOURCES

Visit **abdokids.com** and use this code to access crafts, games, videos, and more!

Abdo Kids Code:
OBK1771